# That Benediction
# is where you are

## The Last Bombay Talks 1985

### J. Krishnamurti

KRISHNAMURTI FOUNDATION INDIA

©—2001 Krishnamurti Foundation Trust Ltd
Brockwood Park, Bramdean
Hampshire SO24 OLQ, England
E-mail: info@brockwood.org.uk

*Published, with permission, by*
Krishnamurti Foundation India
Vasanta Vihar, 124 Greenways Road
Chennai – 600 028.
E-mail: publications@kfionline.org
Website: http://www.kfionline.org

First Edition 2001
Reprinted     2004

Philosophy / Religion
ISBN 81-87326-28-X

*Design and Layout*: Deepa Kamath

*Printed at*
Sudarsan Graphics
27 Neelakanta Mehta Street
T.Nagar, Chennai – 600 017.

# Contents

## Publisher's Note

*That Benediction is where you are* consists of the last series of public talks that Krishnamurti gave in Bombay, in February 1985. He was to go there as usual for talks in 1986 also, but unfortunately he was unable to do so; terminal illness made him go straight from Madras to Ojai, where he died on the 17th of February.

Krishnamurti came to Bombay first in 1921, and gave talks between the years 1924 and 1938. After India's independence in 1947, his association with the city seems to have been almost continuous till 1985. Besides giving public talks, he held a series of discussions with small groups of friends. That was how dialogue as a form of communication started, and many of these dialogues have been compiled in books such as *Tradition and Revolution* and *Exploration into Insight*. He also addressed the staff and students of Bombay University in 1969 and the Indian Institute of Technology in 1984.

Over the decades, Krishnamurti witnessed the alarming growth of Bombay from a wind-swept coastal town to an over-crowded, noisy and polluted metropolis, and he addressed these concerns in many of his talks. However, to him these social problems were but the symptoms of the deeper disorder latent in the psyche of every human being.

Krishnamurti's public talks were generally held during week-ends on the grounds of the J. J. School of Arts which, though located in the heart of the city, had an extensive canopy of trees. The Bombay audiences were perhaps the largest that Krishnamurti ever had anywhere in the world, especially in the 1970s and 1980s. They also represented a wide cross-section of society: scholars, intellectuals, politicians, businessmen, artists, housewives, sannyasis, students, as also Hindus, Muslims, Christians, Buddhists, Jains, and Parsees.

The talks in this book are remarkable for the unusual perspectives and nuances that Krishnamurti offers on the psychological issues he deals with. In the second talk, for instance, he raises various questions regarding insecurity, fragmentation, identification, and fear, but insists on the importance of merely *listening* to the questions and *not doing* anything about them. The listening, he says, is like planting a seed in the earth. 'What is important is to put the question.... Let the question itself answer—like the seed in the earth. Then you will see that the seed flowers and withers. Don't pull it out all the time to see if it is growing.' This idea runs like a refrain throughout the talk.

There is a sense of poignancy in the substance and tone of the last talk, where Krishnamurti urges us to realize that we are wasting our lives by not freeing ourselves from our hurts, conflicts, fears, and sorrows, and by remaining in our narrow world of specialization. This freedom, he says, is the 'first step'. The talk ends on a deeply religious note with his profound observation: 'So, if you give your heart and mind and brain, there is something that is beyond all time. And there is the benediction of that. Not in temples, not in churches, not in mosques. That benediction is where you are.'

Included in this book are a few excerpts from Krishnamurti's writings which capture the beauty of Bombay's waterfront and the atmosphere of the city, as also his sensitivity to people, the rich and the poor.

The sea was very calm and there was hardly a ripple on the white sands. Around the wide bay, to the north, was the town, and to the south were palm trees, almost touching the water. Just visible beyond the bar were the first of the sharks, and beyond them the fishermen's boats, a few logs tied together with stout rope. They were making for a little village south of the palm trees. The sunset was brilliant, not where one would expect it, but in the east; it was a counter-sunset, and the clouds, massive and shapely, were lit with all the colours of the spectrum. It was really quite fantastic, and almost painful to bear. The waters caught the brilliant colours and made a path of exquisite light to the horizon.

(From Chapter 13 'Virtue' in
*Commentaries on Living First Series*)

The sea was very calm that morning, more so than usual, for the wind from the south had ceased blowing, and before the north-easterly winds began, the sea was taking a rest. The sands were bleached by the sun and salt water, and there was a strong smell of ozone, mixed with that of seaweed. There wasn't anyone yet on the beach, and one had the sea to oneself. Large crabs, with one claw much bigger than the other, moved slowly about, watching, with the large claw waving in the air. There were also smaller crabs, the usual kind, that raced to the lapping water, or darted into round holes in the wet sand. Hundreds of sea-gulls stood about, resting and preening themselves. The rim of the sun was just coming out of the sea, and it made a golden path on the still waters. Everything seemed to be waiting for this moment—and how quickly it would pass! The sun continued to climb out of the sea, which was as quiet as a sheltered lake in some deep woods. No woods could contain these waters, they were too restless, too strong and vast; but that morning they were mild, friendly and inviting.

Under a tree above the sands and the blue water, there was going on a life independent of the crabs, the salt water and the sea-gulls. Large, black ants darted about, not making up their minds where to go. They would go up the tree, then suddenly scurry down for no apparent reason. Two or three would impatiently stop, move their heads about, and then, with a fierce burst of energy, go all over a piece of wood which they must have examined hundreds of times before; they would investigate it again with eager curiosity, and lose interest in it a second later. It was very quiet under the tree, though everything about one was very much alive. There was not a breath of air stirring among the leaves, but every leaf was abundant with the beauty and light of the morning. There was an intensity about the tree—not the terrible intensity of reaching, of succeeding, but the intensity of being complete, simple, alone and yet part of the earth. The colours of the leaves, of the few flowers, of the dark trunk, were intensified a thousandfold, and the branches seemed to sustain the heavens. It was incredibly clear, bright and alive in the shade of that single tree.

From Chapter 18 'To Change Society You Must Break Away from It' in *Commentaries on Living Third Series*

---

It was hot and humid and the noise of the very large town filled the air. The breeze from the sea was warm, and there was the smell of tar and petrol. With the setting of the sun, red in the distant waters, it was still unyieldingly hot. The large group that filled the room presently left, and we went out into the street.

The parrots, like bright green flashes of light, were coming home to roost. Early in the morning they flew to the north, where there were orchards, green fields and open country, and in the evening they came back to pass the night in the trees of the city. Their flight was never smooth but always reckless, noisy and brilliant. They never flew straight like other birds, but were forever veering off to the left or the right, or suddenly dropping into a tree. They were the most restless birds in flight, but how beautiful they were with their red beaks and a golden green that was the very glory of light. The vultures, heavy and ugly, circled and settled down for the night on the palm trees.

A man came along playing the flute; he was a servant of some kind. He walked up the hill, still playing, and we followed him; he turned into one of the side-streets, never ceasing to play. It was strange to hear the song of the flute in a noisy city, and its sound penetrated deep into the heart. It was very beautiful, and we followed the flute player for some distance. We crossed several streets and came to a wider one, better lighted. Farther on, a group of people were sitting cross-legged at the side of the road, and the flute player joined them. So did we; and we all sat around while he played. They were mostly chauffeurs, servants, night watchmen, with several children and a dog or two. Cars passed by, one driven by a chauffeur; a lady was inside, beautifully dressed and alone, with the inside light on. Another car drew up; the chauffeur got out and sat down with us. They were all talking and enjoying themselves, laughing and gesticulating, but the song of the flute never wavered, and there was delight.

Presently we left and took a road that led to the sea past the well-lit houses of the rich. The rich have a peculiar atmosphere of their own. However cultured, unobtrusive, ancient and polished, the rich have an impenetrable and assured aloofness, that inviolable certainty and hardness that is difficult to break down. They are not the possessors of wealth, but are possessed by wealth, which is worse than death. Their conceit is philanthropy; they think they are trustees of their wealth; they have charities, create endowments; they are the makers, the builders, the givers. They build churches, temples, but their god is the god of their gold. With so much poverty and degradation, one must have a very thick skin to be rich. Some of them come to question, to argue, to find reality. For the rich as for the poor, it is extremely difficult to find reality. The poor crave to be rich and powerful, and the rich are already caught in the net of their own action; and yet they believe and venture near. They speculate, not only upon the market, but upon the ultimate. They play with both, but are successful only with what is in their hearts. Their beliefs and ceremonies, their hopes and fears have nothing to do with reality, for their hearts are empty. The greater the outward show the greater the inward · poverty.

(From Chapter 7 'The Rich and the Poor' in *Commentaries on Living First Series*)

## TALK 1

*Our brain, which is amazingly free in one
direction, is psychologically a cripple.*

This is a dialogue between us, a conversation between two friends. So this is not a lecture to instruct, inform or guide you. We are going to talk over together many things, certainly not to convince you of anything, or to inform you of new ideas, new concepts, conclusions or ideals. We are going to look together at the whole world as it is, at what is happening not only in this part of the world but also in the rest of the world. Together. And the speaker means together. You and he are going to observe, without any bias, without any prejudice, what is happening globally.

So this is a serious talk, not something intellectual, emotional or devotional. So we must exercise our brains. We must have scepticism, doubt; we must question and not accept anything that anybody says—including all your gurus and sacred books. We have come to a crisis in the world. The crisis is not merely economic; rather it is psychological.

1

We have lived on this earth for over a million years and, during that long period of time, we have passed through every kind of catastrophe, every kind of war. Civilizations have disappeared; so have cultures that shaped the behaviour of human beings. We have had a great many leaders, political and religious, with all the tricks that they have played on human beings. And after this enormous evolution of the human brain, we are what we have been—rather primitive, barbarous, cruel, and always preparing for war. Every nation now is storing up armaments. And we human beings are caught in this wheel of time. We have not changed very much; we are still barbarians, with all kinds of superstitions and beliefs. At the end of it all, where are we?

Please, we are talking over things together. It is not that the speaker is explaining all this; it is so obvious. You and the speaker are together examining very carefully, diligently, what we have become, what we are. And we ask: Will time change us? Will time, that is, another fifty thousand or a million years change the human mind, the human brain? Or is time not important at all? We are going to talk about all these things.

Human beings are wounded psychologically. Human beings throughout the world are caught in great sorrow, pain, suffering, loneliness, and despair. And the brain has created the most extraordinary things, ideologically, technologically, religiously. The brain is extraordinarily capable. But that capacity is very limited. Technologically we are advancing at an extraordinary speed. But psychologically, inwardly, we are very primitive, barbarous, cruel, thoughtless, careless, and indifferent to what is happening. We are indifferent not only to the corruption that goes on environmentally but also to the corruption that goes on in the name of religion, in the name of politics, business, and so on. Corruption is not just passing money under the table or smuggling goods into the country. Corruption begins where there is self-interest. Where there is self-interest, that is the origin of corruption.

Are we thinking together, or are you merely listening to the speaker? Are we going together as two friends, taking a long journey—a journey into the global world, a journey into ourselves: into what we are, what we have become, and why we have become what we are. And we need to take this journey together. It is not that the speaker takes the journey and points out to you the map, the road, and the way. But, rather, we are together, and the speaker means together. For he is not a guru. One should not follow anybody in the world of thought, in the world of the psyche. We have depended so much on others to help us. And we are not helping you. Let us be very clear on that point: the speaker is not helping you because you have had helpers galore. And we have not been able to stand alone, think out things for ourselves; we have not been able to look at the world and our relationship to the world, and see whether we are individuals at all or part of humanity. We have not exercised our brains, which are so extraordinarily capable. We have expended our energy, our capacity, our intellectual understanding in one direction only— the technological. But we have never understood human behaviour and why we are as we are after this long period of evolution.

And as the speaker said just now, he is not helping you; we are together looking, under- standing. Of course, we need the help of a physician or a surgeon. We depend on governments, however rotten they are. We have to depend on the postman, and the milkman, and so on. But to ask for help through prayer, through meditation seems so utterly futile. We have had such help; we have had thousands of gurus and thousands of books— so-called religious and non-religious. And in spite of them all we are helpless. We may earn a lot of money, have big houses, cars, and so on, but psychologically, inwardly, subjectively, we are almost helpless because we have depended on other people to tell us what to do, what to think. So, please, the speaker is saying most respectfully, seriously, and earnestly that he is not trying to help you. On the contrary, we are together.

So you and the speaker have to investigate all this: our relationship to the world, which is becoming more and more complex, our relationship to each other however intimate it might be, our relationship to an ideal, our relationship to our gurus, and to so-called God. We have to inquire seriously, deeply, into the quality of a brain that comprehends, or has an insight into the whole outer as well as the psychological world in which we live. It must be clear that we are not trying to point out a way, a method, a system, or in any way trying to help you. On the contrary. We are independent human beings. This is not a cruel or indifferent statement. We are like two friends talking over together, trying to understand the world: the environment, all the complications of the economic world, the separate religions, and separate nations. Friendship means that we are not trying to persuade, coerce or impress each other. We are friends and, therefore, there is a certain quality of affection, understanding, exchange. We are in that position.

So we first begin with what our brain is. The speaker is not a brain specialist, but he has talked with brain specialists. The brain, which is inside the skull, is a most extraordinary instrument. It has acquired tremendous knowledge about almost everything. It has invented the most incredible things like the computer, the means of quick communication, and instruments of war. And here it is entirely free to investigate, invent, research. It starts with knowledge, and accumulates more and more knowledge. If a certain theory does not work, it is dropped. But the brain is not equally free to inquire into the self. It is conditioned, shaped, programmed—to be a Hindu, a Muslim, a Christian, a Buddhist, and so on. Like a computer, the human brain is programmed—that you must have war, that you belong to a certain group, that your roots are in this part of the world, and so on. This is correct; this is not an exaggeration. All of us are programmed by tradition, by the constant repetition in newspapers and magazines, by thousands of years of pressure. The brain is free in one direction: in the world of technology. But that very brain, which is so extraordinarily capable, is limited by its own self-interest. Our brain, which is amazingly free in one direction, is psychologically a cripple.

Is it possible for the human brain to be entirely free so that there is tremendous energy?—not to do more mischief, not to have more money, or power—though you must have money—but to inquire, to find out a way of life in which there is no fear, no loneliness, and no sorrow, and to inquire into the nature of death, meditation, and truth. Is it possible for the human brain, which has been conditioned for thousands of years, to be entirely free? Or must human beings everlastingly be slaves, never knowing what freedom is?—not freedom in the abstract but freedom from conflict, because we live in conflict. One fact common to all human beings—from childhood till they die—is this constant struggle, seeking security and therefore never finding it, or being insecure, wanting security. So is it possible for human beings in the modern world with all its complexities to live without a shadow of conflict? Because conflict distorts the brain, lessens its capacity, its energy, and the brain soon wears itself out. You can observe in yourself as you grow older this perpetual conflict.

What is conflict? Please do not wait for me to answer it; that is no fun at all. Ask yourself that question, and give your mind to find out what is the nature of conflict. Conflict exists, surely, when there is duality: 'me' and 'you', my wife separate from me, the division between the meditator and meditation. So, as long as there is division between nationalities, between religions, between people, between the ideal and the fact, between 'what is' and 'what should be', there must be conflict. That is a law. Wherever there is separation, the sense of division as the Arab and the Jew, the Hindu and the Muslim, the son and the father, and so on, there must be conflict. That is a fact. That division is the 'more': 'I do not know, but give me a few years and I will know.' I hope you understand all this.

Who has created this division between 'what is' and 'what should be'? There is the division between so-called God, if there is such an entity, and yourself, and the division between wanting peace and being in conflict. This is the actual reality of our daily life. And the speaker is asking, as you must be asking too: Who has created this division, not only externally but also inwardly? Please ask yourselves this question. Who is responsible for all this mess, this endless struggle, endless pain, loneliness, despair, and a sense of sorrow from which man seems to have never escaped? Who is responsible for all this? Who is responsible for the society in which we live? There is immense poverty in this country. Do you understand all this, or you have never thought about it at all? Or are you so occupied with your own meditations, with your own gods, with your own problems, that you have never looked at all this, never asked?

There are several things involved in all this. Those who are fairly intelligent, fairly aware, and sensitive have always sought an egalitarian society. They have asked: Can there be equal opportunity, no class difference, so that there is no division between the worker and the manager, the carpenter and the politician? So we ask: Is there justice in the world? There have been revolutions—French, Bolshevik—which have tried to establish a society where there is equality, justice, and goodness. But they have not succeeded at all. On the contrary, they have gone back to the old pattern in a different setting. So you have to inquire not only into why human beings live in perpetual conflict and sorrow, and why they search for security, but also into the nature of justice. Is there any justice at all in the world? Is there? You are clever, another is not. You have got all the privileges, and another has none whatsoever. You live in a palatial house, and another lives in a hut, having hardly one meal a day. So is there justice at all? Is it not important to find out for oneself and, therefore, help humanity. (I am sorry, I do not mean 'help'; I withdraw that word.) To understand the nature of justice and find out if there is any justice at all, you must inquire very, very deeply into the nature of sorrow, and whether there can be no self-interest at all. And also we should inquire into what is freedom and what is goodness.

The society in which we live is created by every human being through his greed, envy, aggression, and the search for security. We have created the society in which we live, and then we become slaves to that society. Do you understand all this? We human beings out of fear, out of loneliness, and in our search for security—never understanding what insecurity is but always wanting security—have created our culture, our society, our religions, our gods. To come back: Who has created this division? Because where there is division, there is conflict. That is an absolute certainty. Think it out, sir. Is it not thought that has divided the world as the Christians, the Buddhists, the Jews, the Arabs, the Hindus, and the Muslims? Is it not thought?

Then we ask: What is thought? Thought is the action by which we live. Thought is our central factor of action. Right? Thought—by which we make money; thought which separates me and you, the husband and the wife, the ideal and 'what is'. Then, what is thought? What is thinking? Is not thinking the activity of memory? Please, sirs, do not accept a thing that the speaker is saying. You must have this quality of doubt; doubt your own experiences, your own ideas. The speaker is saying as a friend—to whom you can listen or not listen as you please—that thought has created this division. Thought has been responsible for wars, has been responsible for all the gods that man has invented. Thought has been responsible for putting man on the moon, for creating the computer and all the extraordinary things of the technological world. And thought is also responsible for the division and conflict between 'what is' and 'what should be'. The 'what should be' is the ideal; it is something to be achieved, something to be gained, away from 'what is'. For example, human beings are violent. That is an obvious fact. Even after a long period of time, man is not free of violence. But he has invented non-violence. He has invented it and is pursuing it. He would acknowledge that he is violent—if he is at all honest. But in the pursuit of the ideal called non-violence, he is sowing the seeds of violence all the time. Naturally. This is a fact.

This country has talked a great deal about non-violence. This is rather shameful because we are all violent people. Violence is not merely physical; it is also imitation, conformity, moving away from 'what is'. So violence can end completely in the human mind, the human heart, only when there is no opposite. The opposite is the non-violence which is not real; it is another escape from violence. If you do not escape, then there is only violence. But you have not been able to face that fact. You are always running away from the fact, finding excuses, finding economic reasons, finding innumerable methods to overcome it, but there is still violence. The very overcoming is a part of violence.

So, to face violence, you must give attention to it, and not run away from it. You must see what it is, see the violence between man and woman, sexually and in other ways. Is there not violence when you are seeking more and more, 'becoming' more and more? So to look at violence and remain with it; do not run away from it, or try to suppress it, or transcend it—all that implies conflict. To live with it, look at it, in fact, treasure it, and not translate it according to your want, likes and dislikes. Just to look and observe with great attention. When you give attention to something completely, it is like turning on a bright light, and then you see all the qualities, the subtleties, the implications—the whole world—of violence. When you see something very clearly, it is gone. But you refuse to see things clearly.

So we are asking: Who has created this conflict of human beings with each other, with the environment, with the gods, with everything? Have you ever considered why you think you are an individual? Are you an individual? Or have you been programmed to think you are an individual? Your consciousness is like every other human being's consciousness. You suffer, you are lonely, you are afraid, and you seek pleasure and avoid pain. It is so with every human being on this earth. This is a fact, a psychological fact. You may be tall, you may be dark, you may be fair, but those are all external frills, of climate, food, and so on. And culture too is external. But psychologically, subjectively, our consciousness is common, one with all other human beings. You may not like it, but that is a fact. So psychologically you are not separate from the rest of humanity. You *are* humanity. Do not say 'Yes'; it has no meaning merely accepting it as an idea. It is a tremendous fact that you are the rest of mankind, and not somebody separate. You may have a better brain, more wealth, more cunning, better looks. But put aside all that for they are all surface things, they are frills. Inwardly, every human being on this earth is one with you in sorrow. Do you realize what that means? It implies that when you say you are the rest of humanity, you have tremendous responsibility. It implies that you have great affection, love, compassion, and not some silly idea that 'we are all one'.

So we must inquire into what is thinking and why thinking has become so extraordinarily important. Thinking cannot exist without memory. If there was no memory, there would be no thought. Our brains—which are one with all the rest of humanity, and not separate little brains—are conditioned by knowledge, by memory. And knowledge, memory, is based on experience, both in the scientific world and the subjective world. Our experiences, however subtle, however spiritual, and however personal, are always limited. So our knowledge, which is the outcome of experience, is also limited. And we are adding more and more; and where there is addition, that which is being added to is limited. So we are saying that experience being limited, knowledge is always limited, either now, in the past, or in the future.

And knowledge means memory—the memory held either in the computer or in the brain. So the brain is memory. And that memory directs thought. This is a fact. So thought is always limited. Right? This is logical, rational, not something invented; this is so. Experience is limited. Therefore knowledge is limited.

Then we ask: Is there any other activity which is not divisive, which is not fragmentary, which does not break up? Is there a holistic activity that can never break up—as me and you? It is division which creates conflict. Now, how are you going to find this out for yourselves, seeing that thought is divisive, that thought creates conflict, that thought has created the society and then set you apart from the society which you have created? Thought is the only instrument we have had so far. You may say that there is another instrument which is intuition. But that can be irrational; you can invent anything and live in an illusion.

So we are asking, very seriously, whether one has understood the nature of thought and whether there is any other action or a way of living which is never fragmentary, never broken up as the world and me, and me and the world. Is there such a state of brain, or a state of non-brain, which is completely holistic, whole?

You will find out if you are serious, if you are free. You have to throw away everything that you have accumulated, not physically—please do not throw away your bank account; you won't any-how—but psychologically put away everything that you have collected. That is going to be very difficult. That means there must be freedom. You know, the word 'freedom' etymologically also means love.

When there is freedom, boundless and at such enormous depths, there is also love. And to find that out, or to come upon that holistic way of living in which there is no self-interest, there must be freedom from friction, from conflict in relationship.

We live by relationship. You may live in the Himalayas, or in a monastery, or by yourself in a little hut or a palace, but you cannot live without relationship. Relationship implies 'to be related to', 'to be in contact with', not just physically or sexually, but to be completely in contact with another. But we are never completely related to another. Even in the most intimate relationship—man and woman— each is pursuing his or her own particular ambition, particular fulfilment, and one's own way of living as opposed to the other, like two parallel lines never meeting. In this relationship there is always conflict. Face the fact.

And what creates conflict between two human beings? In your relationship with your wife, with your husband, with your children—which is the most intimate relationship—what is it that creates conflict? Ask yourselves, sirs. Is it not that you have an image about your wife and she has an image about you? That image has been built very, very carefully over a short period or a very long period. This constant recording of the brain in relationship with another is the picture that you have created about your wife or your husband. And that picture divides. And especially when you are living in the same house with all the turmoil, you escape from that by becoming a monk or whatever it is. But you have your own problems there too, your own desires, your own pursuits, which again become a conflict.

So can you live without a single image of another? No image at all. Have you ever tried it? See the logic of it, the sanity of it that as long as the picture-making machinery goes on, recording the insult or the flattery, it creates an image about another, and that image is a divisive factor. So is it possible to live without a single image? Then you will find out what true relationship is because then there will be no conflict at all in relationship. And that is absolutely necessary if one is to understand the limitation of thought and inquire into a holistic way of living that is completely non-fragmentary.

Another factor in our lives is that from childhood we are trained to have problems. When we are sent to school, we have to learn how to write, how to read, and all the rest of it. How to write becomes a problem to the child. Please follow this carefully. Mathematics becomes a problem, history becomes a problem, as does chemistry. So the child is educated, from childhood, to live with problems— the problem of God, problem of a dozen things. So our brains are conditioned, trained, educated to live with problems. From childhood we have done this. What happens when a brain is educated in problems? It can never solve problems; it can only create more problems. When a brain that is trained to have problems, and to live with problems, solves one problem, in the very solution of that problem, it creates more problems. From childhood we are trained, educated to live with problems and, therefore, being centred in problems, we can never solve any problem completely. It is only the free brain that is not conditioned to problems that can solve problems. It is one of our constant burdens to have problems all the time. Therefore our brains are never quiet, free to observe, to look.

So we are asking: Is it possible not to have a single problem but to face problems? But to understand those problems, and to totally resolve them, the brain must be free. See the logic of it because logic is necessary, reason is necessary, and only then can you go beyond reason, beyond logic. But if you are not logical, step by step by step, then you may deceive yourself all along and end up in some kind of illusion. So to find out a way of living in which you can face problems, resolve them, and not be caught in them requires a great deal of observation, attention, and awareness to see that you never deceive yourself for a second.

First, there must be order. And order begins only when there are no problems, when there is freedom—not freedom to do what you like; that is not freedom at all. To choose between this guru and that guru, or between this book and that book— that is merely another form of confusion. Where there is choice, there is no freedom. And choice exists only when the brain is confused. When the brain is clear, then there is no choice, but only direct perception and right action.

*2 February 1985*

## TALK 2

*Thought and time are always together. They are not two separate movements.*

May we go on with what we were talking about yesterday evening? This is really not a talk, but a conversation between us, a conversation between two friends—friends who have known each other for a very long time, who are not trying to impress each other or convince each other about anything; we are just friends. We may play golf together, take walks, look at the sky, the trees, the green lawns and the beautiful mountains. And we are talking over our intimate problems—problems which we have not been able to solve, issues that are confusing, living as we do in the modern world, with all its difficulties, turmoil, and vulgarity. We are concerned about what human beings are going to become and why, after a million years, they are what they are now: unreasonable, super-stitious, believing in anything, gullible, and caught in organizations.

So you and the speaker are going to talk over things together. That is, you do not merely listen to the speaker, but enter into the spirit, into the inquiry. So you have to exercise your brains as much as possible. Do not accept anything he says. Be sceptical, question, inquire and, if you will, together we shall take a long journey, not only outwardly but inwardly, into the whole psychological world: the world of thought, the world of sorrow, the world of fear and travail.

This is not a lecture to inform or instruct you. But together we are going to have a dialogue, a conversation, without holding on to our own particular beliefs or convictions, experiences or superstitions, but exchanging, changing as we go along. So there is no question of doing any propaganda, of trying to convince you of anything at all. On the contrary, we must doubt, question, inquire and, as friends, listen to each other.

Listening is an art which very few of us are capable of. We never *actually* listen. The word has a sound and when we do not listen to the sound, we interpret it, try to translate it into our own particular language or tradition. We never listen acutely, without any distortion. So, the speaker suggests, respectfully, that you so listen and not interpret what he says. When you tell a rather exciting story to a little boy, he listens with a tremendous sense of curiosity and energy. He wants to know what is going to happen, and he waits excitedly to the very end. But we grown-up people have lost all that curiosity, the energy to find out, that energy which is required to see very clearly things as they are, without any distortion. We never listen to each other. You never listen to your wife, do you? You know her much too well, or she you. There is no sense of deep appreciation, friendship, amity, which would make you listen to each other, whether you like it or not. But if you do listen so completely, that very act of listening is a great miracle.

That listening, like seeing, observing, is very important. We never observe. We observe things that are convenient, friendly. We observe only if there is a reward or punishment. I do not know if you have noticed that our whole upbringing, all our education and our daily life is based on one principle: reward and punishment. We meditate in order to be rewarded, we 'progress' in order to be rewarded, and so on. When we seek a reward, physical or psychological, in that search for a reward there is also the punishment—if that reward is not satisfying. So could we listen to each other *per se*, for itself, not for something else? Could we listen, as we would listen to  marvellous music or to the song of a bird, with our hearts, with our minds, with all the energy that we have? Then we can go very far.

Most human beings, all of us, seek security, and it takes many forms. Security is very important. If we are not secure, both physically and psychologically, our brains cannot function adequately, fully, energetically. We must have security. But physical security is denied to millions and millions of people; they have hardly one meal a day. And we, the so-called educated, well-to-do people are all the time seeking, consciously or otherwise, a kind of security which would give us complete satisfaction. We want security, and it is necessary both biologically and psychologically. But in our search for security we never inquire into what is insecurity. If we can find out together what insecurity is and why we are insecure, then in its very unfolding, security comes about naturally.

So what is insecurity? Why are we insecure in our relationship to each other? There is tremendous disturbance, turmoil and agony in the external world, and each one wants his own place, his own security, and wants to escape from this terrible state of insecurity. So, can we, together inquire into why we are insecure?—not into what security is because your security may be an illusion. Your security may be in some romantic concept, in some image, tradition, or in a family and name. What does that word 'insecure' mean? In your relationship to your wife or husband, there is not a sense of complete security. There is always this background, this feeling that everything is not quite right. So inquire with me into why human beings are insecure. Is it about not having a job? In a country like this, which is overpopulated, there are probably ten thousand people for one job. Don't you know all this, or am I inventing it? If we were not insecure, we would not talk about gods, we would not talk about security. Because we are insecure, we seek the opposite.

Have you ever listened to sound? Sound! The universe is filled with sound. The earth is full of sound. And we seek silence. We meditate to find some kind of peace or some kind of silence. But if we understood sound, in the very hearing of the sound there would be silence. Silence is not separate from sound. But we do not understand that because we never listen to sound. Have you ever sat under a tree when the air is very still, quiet, when not a leaf is dancing? Have you ever sat under a tree like that and listened to the sound of the tree? If there was no silence, there would be no sound. So the sound of insecurity—the very sound—makes us seek security because we have never listened to the sound of insecurity. If we listened to all the implications of insecurity, to the whole movement of insecurity —which makes us invent gods, rituals and all that— then out of that insecurity there comes about, naturally, security. But if you pursue security as something separate from insecurity, then you are in conflict.

You know, of an evening when the sky is clear— not in Bombay—and there is only one star in the sky, and there is absolute silence, if you listen to that silence, in that silence there is sound. And there is no separation between sound and silence; they both go together. In the same way, understand insecurity, its causation. The cause of insecurity is our own limited, broken-up psychological state. But when there is a way of living that is holistic, then there is no such thing as security or insecurity.

So, if you will, we shall talk over together: What is a holistic way of life? The word 'whole' means complete, a state in which there is no fragmentation—no fragments such as a businessman, an artist, a poet, a religious person, and so on. But we are constantly categorizing people as communists, socialists, capitalists, and so on.

Our lives, if you observe closely, are broken up. Our lives are fragmented. And we have to understand why we human beings, who have lived on this marvellous earth for millions of years, are so fragmented, so broken up? As we said yesterday, one of the main causes of this breaking up is that the brain is a slave to thought, and thought is limited. Wherever there is limitation, there must be fragmentation. When I am concerned with myself, with my progress, my fulfilment, my happiness, my problems, I have broken up the whole structure of humanity into the 'me'. So one of the factors of why human beings are fragmented is thought. And another of the factors is time.

Have you ever considered what time is? According to the scientists who are concerned with it, time is a series of movements. So movement is time. And time is not only by the watch, chronological: time as the sun rising and the sun setting, the darkness of the night and the brightness of the morning. There is also psychological time, inward time: 'I am this, but I will become that'; 'I don't know mathematics, but one day I will learn all about it.' That requires time. To learn a new language requires a great deal of time. There is time to learn, to memorize, to develop a skill, and there is also time as the self-centred entity saying, 'I will become something else.' The 'becoming' psychologically also implies time. We are inquiring into not only the time to learn a skill but also the time which we have developed as a process of achievement. You do not know how to meditate, so you sit cross-legged and learn how to control your thoughts so that one day you will achieve what meditation is supposed to be. So you practise, practise, practise, and thus you become mechanical. That is, whatever you practise makes you mechanical.

So time is the past, the present, and the future. Time that is the past is all the memories, all the experiences, knowledge, and all that human beings have achieved. All that which remains in the brain as memory is the past. That is simple. The past— the memories, the knowledge, the experiences, the tendencies—the background is operating now. So you are the past. And the future is what you are now, perhaps modified. The future is the past modified. See this, please understand. The past, modified in the present, is the future. So if there is no radical change in the present, tomorrow will be the same as what you are today. So the future is now—not the future needed for acquiring knowledge, but the psychological future. That is, the psyche, the 'me', the self, is the past, is memory. That memory modifies itself now, and goes on. So the future and the past are in the present. All time— the past, the present and the future—is contained in the now. This is not complicated please, it is logical. So if you do not change now, instantly, the future will be what you are now, what you have been. So is it possible to change radically, fundamentally, now?—not in the future.

We are the past. There is no question about it. And that past gets modified by reaction, by challenges, in various ways. And that becomes the future. Look, you have had a civilization in this country for three to five thousand years. That is the past. But modern circumstances demand that you break away from the past, and so you have no culture any more. You may talk about your past culture and enjoy its past fame, but that past is blown up, scattered by the present demands, the present challenge. And that challenge, that demand is changing it into an economic entity.

So all past and future is in the now. So all time is in the now. And we are saying that thought and time are the major causes of fragmented human beings. Also, we want roots, identification. We want to be identified with a group, a guru, a family, a nation, and so on. And the threat of war is a major factor in our lives. War may destroy our psychological roots, and therefore we are willing to kill others. So these are the major factors of our fragmented lives.

Now, do you listen to the truth of it, or merely to a description of what is being said and, therefore, carry the description and not the truth, the idea and not the fact? For instance, the speaker says, 'All time is now.' If you understand that, it is a most marvellous truth. Do you listen to that as a series of words, as an idea, as an abstraction of the truth, or do you capture the truth of it? Which is it that you are doing? Do you see, live with the fact? Or do you make an abstraction of the fact, an idea, and then pursue the idea and not the fact? That is what the intellect does. Intellect is necessary, but probably we have very little intellect anyhow because we have given ourselves over to somebody. So when you hear a statement like, 'All time is now', or 'You are the entire humanity because your consciousness is one with all the others', how do you listen to it? Do you make an abstraction, an idea, of it? Or do you listen to the truth, to the fact of it, the depth of it, to the sense of immensity involved in it? Ideas are not immense, but a fact has got tremendous possibility.

So a holistic life is not possible when there is thought, time, and the desire for identification and for roots. They prevent a way of living that is whole, complete. You hear the statement, and your question then will be, 'How shall I stop thinking?' It is a natural question, isn't it? You know that time is necessary to learn a skill, a language, or a technical subject. But you have also just begun to realize that the 'becoming', the moving from 'what is' to 'what should be', involves time, and that it may be totally wrong, it may not be true. So you begin to question. Or do you just say, 'I don't understand what you are talking about but I will go along with it'? Which is actually what is taking place. Honesty, like humility, is one of the most important things. When a vain man cultivates humility, that humility is part of vanity. But humility has nothing to do with vanity, with pride. It is a state of the mind that says, 'I don't know what I am, let me inquire', and never says, 'I know.'

Now, you have listened to the fact that all time is now. You may agree or you may not agree. That is a dreadful thing—agreeing and disagreeing. Why should we agree or disagree? The fact is that the sun rises in the east; you don't agree or disagree with it. So can we put aside our conditioning of agreeing and disagreeing so that we both can look at facts, so that there is no division between those who agree and those who do not? Then there is only seeing things as they are. You may say, 'I don't see', but that is a different matter. Then we can go into why you don't see. But when we enter into the area of agreement and disagreement, we become more and more confused.

The speaker has said our lives are fragmented, our ways of thinking are fragmented. You are a businessman, you earn lots and lots of money and then you build a temple or give to charity. See the contradiction in it. We are never deeply honest with ourselves—not honest in order to be something else or to understand something else. But to be clear and to have an absolute sense of honesty is to have no illusions. If you tell a lie, you tell a lie and you know it and say, 'I have told a lie', and do not cover it up. When you are angry, you are angry and you say that you are angry. You do not find causes, explanations for it, or try to get rid of it. This is absolutely necessary if you are going to inquire into much deeper things, as we are doing now. Not make a fact into an idea but to remain with the fact—that requires very clear perception.

Now, having heard all this you will say, 'Yes, I understand this logically, intellectually.' And you will ask: 'How am I to relate what I have understood logically, intellectually, to what I have heard? What is the truth?' So you have already created a division between intellectual understanding and action. Do you see this? So listen, *just* listen. Don't do anything about it. Don't ask, 'How am I to get something?' 'How am I to put an end to thought and time?'— which you cannot. That would be absurd because you are the result of time and thought. You will just go round and round in circles. But listen, don't react, don't ask, 'how?' but actually listen—as you would

listen to some lovely music or to the call of a bird—
to the statement that all time is in the now and that
thought is a movement. Thought and time are always
together. They are not two separate movements, but
one constant movement. That is a fact. Listen to it.

Then, you want to be identified, and that is one
of the causes of fragmentation of our lives, like time
and thought. Also, you want security and therefore
you take roots. So these are the factors of fragmentation. Listen to this. Don't *do* anything. Now,
if you listen very carefully, that very listening creates
its own energy. If you listen to the fact of what is
being said and do not react—because you are just
listening to it—that implies the gathering of all your
energy to listen. That means giving tremendous
attention to listening. And that very listening
breaks down the factors or the causes of fragmentation. If you *do* something, then you are
acting upon the fact. But if there is an observation,
without distortion, without prejudice, then that
very observation, that very perception which is great
attention, burns away the sense of time, thought,
and all the rest of it.

And also one of the factors of our lives, in which
we live in fragmentation, is fear. That is a common

human fact. Human beings, right from the beginning of time, have been frightened. And they have never solved the problem. If you were not frightened at all, there would be no gods, no rituals, no prayers. It is our fear that has created all the gods, all the deities, and the gurus with their absurdities. So can we go into the question of why human beings live in fear and whether it is possible to be free of it entirely, not occasionally, not sporadically? Can you be aware of the objects of fear and also the inward causes of fear? You may say, 'I am not afraid', but all your background is structured on fear.

What is fear? Are you not afraid? If you are really honest, for a change, will you not say, 'I am afraid'? Afraid of death. Afraid of losing a job. Afraid of your wife or husband. Afraid of public opinion. Afraid of not being recognized by your guru as a great disciple. Afraid of the dark. Afraid of so many things. We are not talking about the objects of fear, fear *of* something. We are inquiring into fear *per se*, in itself. So we are asking: What is the cause of fear, and what is fear without a cause? Is there such a thing as fear without a cause? Or does the word 'fear', the sound of fear, evokes in us fear? For example, when you hear the word 'communism', you would react to it, if you are a capitalist or even if you are a socialist. And when you hear the word 'fear', you react to it, don't you? Of course you do. Now, does the word create the fear, or is the word different from the fear? We are asking, is the word 'fear' different from the fact, or does the word create the fact? One must be clear about this. If there was no such word as 'fear', would there be fear? You see, sir, the word 'love' is not that flame. Similarly, the word 'fear' may not be the actual, the sense of being gripped, of living in a state of nervousness. You know what fear does to people. They live in darkness, they are all the time frightened, frightened, frightened, and their lives get shattered. So we are saying that the word is not the fact, the word is not the thing. That must be quite clear. So what is the cause of fear?

Now, just a minute. The speaker has asked you this question: What is the cause of fear? How do you listen to it? That question has a vitality of its own, an energy of its own. It is a very serious question, not merely an intellectual one. If you remain with the question and not try to find an answer, the question itself begins to unfold. Suppose I tell you in all seriousness, 'I love you.'

I say that with my heart. How do you listen to it? Do you listen to it, or do all your reactions come into it? Perhaps, you have never loved at all. You may be married, have sex, children, but you may not know what love is. Probably you don't. This may be a fact. If you loved, there would be no images, no divisions. So what is the cause of fear? If I may most respectfully suggest, listen to it. Put that question to yourself and do not try to find an answer. Because if you try to find an answer—which is to find out the cause and then end it—it means that 'you' are different from fear. But are you different from fear? Or you *are* fear? If you are greedy, is the greed different from you? When you are angry, is anger different from you? You *are* anger, you *are* greed. So you *are* fear. Of course. Can you admit—not admit but see the fact—that anger is you, greed is you, fear is you? But now you have separated yourself from fear and so you say, 'I must do something about it.' And you have done something about it for fifty thousand years; you have invented gods, puja, and all the rest of it.

So listen to the question and don't react. Don't ask 'how?' The word 'how?' must disappear completely from your minds. Otherwise you would be asking for help. Then you become dependent on somebody. Then you lose all your vitality, independence, and sense of stability. So will you put this question to yourself and not expect an answer? Put the question. You have planted a seed in the earth, and if the seed is alive it will go through concrete. Haven't you seen a blade of grass in the pavement? What extraordinary vitality that blade of grass has to break through the heavy cement! In the same way, if you put this question to yourself and hold it, then you will see the cause. The cause is very simple. I can explain it, but that is not the point for the moment. What is important is to put the question because you are serious and you want to find out. Let the question itself answer—like the seed in the earth. Then you will see that the seed flowers and withers. Don't pull it out all the time to see if it is growing. As you have planted a seed in the earth, so we have planted in our hearts and minds the sense of what is fear. But if you keep on pulling at it, and asking it, then you lose energy. But if you leave the question alone and live with it, then you will see that there is a cause for fear—not the word, not the explanation but the actual truth of it. The cause of fear is thought and time: 'I have a job but I might lose it tomorrow.' 'I have lived with pain and it is gone now, but I am afraid it might come back.' Don't you know all this?

So time is the future and the past, as I explained now. And also thought. Thought and time are the two factors of fear. You cannot do anything about it. Don't ask, 'How am I to stop thinking?' It is too silly a question. Because you have got to think—to go from here to your house, to drive a car, to speak a language. But time may not be necessary at all psychologically, inwardly. So we are saying fear exists because of the two major factors of time and thought, in which is involved reward and punishment.

Now, I have heard this statement made by you. And I have listened to it so immensely because it is a tremendous problem which man has not solved at all and which, therefore, is creating havoc in the world. I have listened to you, listened to the statement. And you have also told me: Don't do anything about it; just put the question and live with it, as a woman bears the seed in her womb. So you have put the question. Let that question flower. In the flowering of that question, there is also the withering away of that question. It is not the flowering and then the ending—the very flowering is the ending. Do you understand what we are talking about?

Sirs, learn the art of listening, to your wife, to your husband. Listen to the man in the street—his hunger, his poverty, his desperation, and the lack of love. Listen to it. When you listen, at that moment you have no problems, you have no turmoil. You are just *listening* and, therefore, there is no time in the act of listening.

*3 February 1985*

# TALK 3

*Sorrow is part of your self-interest, part of your egotistic, self-centred activity.*

We were talking last week about a holistic life—a way of living that is not fragmented, not broken up, as our lives are. We went into the question fairly deeply. We saw what the causes of this fragmentation were, the various factors in our social, moral, and religious life that have broken us up as Hindus, Muslims, Christians, Buddhists, and so on. Religions have been greatly responsible for this catastrophe. We also talked about time, time being the past—all the memories, the accumulated experiences, and so on—modified by the present and continuing into the future. That is our life. We have existed on this earth, according to the biologists and the archaeologists, for over three-and-a-half million years. During that long period of so-called evolution, we have accumulated enormous memory. We also talked about the limitation of memory and thought, and about how that limitation has broken up the world geographically, nationally, and religiously.

As we said the other day, this is not a lecture to inform or instruct you. You are not listening, if I may most respectfully point out, to a series of ideas or conclusions. But rather you and the speaker are taking a journey together like two friends talking over not only their family problems but also the world problems. So it is as much your responsibility to listen carefully, as it is that of the speaker to say things clearly, so that both of us understand what we are talking about. We are going to talk over together about order and disorder, pleasure, love, sorrow, and death. These are all rather complicated problems which we all have to face in our daily lives, whether we are rich or poor. We have got to face this problem of existence.

Our lives, our daily lives are in disorder. Which means contradiction—saying one thing and doing another, believing in something but actually moving in a direction totally different from what we believe. This contradiction creates disorder. I wonder whether we are at all aware of this problem. Apparently, there is going to be more and more disorder in the world on account of bad governments and economic and social conditions. There is always the threat of war, which is becoming more and more imminent, more and more pressing, and governments all over the world, even the tiniest nations, are buying armaments. So throughout the world there is great disorder. And our daily lives are also in disorder, though we are always pursuing order. We want order, because without order human beings will inevitably destroy themselves.

I hope we are sharing this question, thinking together, observing together, listening together, having a dialogue in which you are participating. It is not a matter of gathering a few ideas and conclusions, but together we must find out why we live in disorder and whether there can be total order in our lives and therefore in society.

Society is brought about by us. It is put together by us, by our greed, our ambition, our envy, and the concept of individual freedom. This sense of individuality has brought about a great deal of disorder. Please, we are not attacking anything; we are merely observing what is going on in the world. In our lives, as we live it now after all these million years, there is still disorder. And we have always sought order, because without order we cannot possibly function freely, holistically. So we must find out what is order—not a blueprint, not something we put into a framework and follow. Order is something that is active, living; it does not conform to a pattern, whether the pattern be idealistic, historical or dialectical conclusions, or religious sanctions. Religions throughout the world have laid down certain laws, certain sanctions, and commandments, but human beings have not followed them at all. So we can put aside all those ideological conclusions and religious beliefs, which have nothing to do with our daily existence. We may conform to and follow certain laws laid down by religions, but that only brings about great bigotry, and so on.

What is order? Is it possible to find out what is order when our brains are confused and disorderly? So we must first find out what is disorder, not what is order. Because when there is no disorder, there will naturally be order. Right? One of the causes of this disorder, perhaps the major cause, is conflict. Where there is conflict—not only between man and woman but also between nations, between religious beliefs and faiths—there must be disorder.

Another major cause of disorder is this concept, this illusion that we are all individuals. As we said in the previous talks, you must question, doubt what the speaker is saying. Do not accept anything from anybody, but question, investigate, and not resist. If you merely resist what is being said, which may be true or false, then our conversation comes to an end. When two people are talking over together their problems, and if one is resisting, then conversation ends. So we must go into the question whether we live in this illusion that we are all separate individuals. The communist theory, as most of you perhaps know, is that we are the result of the environment, and so if we change the environment, human beings will change. This is altogether absurd as the Russian totalitarianism has shown very clearly; the dominance of the few, the control of thinking, and so on have not brought about the end of individuality as was hoped. On the contrary. So this is one of the major causes of disorder in our lives—each one thinking he is free, each one thinking of his own fulfil-ment, his own desires, his own ambitions, his own private pleasures. We are going to find out whether individuality is a fact or a long-established, res-pectable illusion. May we go into this together without accepting or denying? It is foolish to say, 'I agree with you' or 'I disagree with you.' You don't 'agree' or 'disagree' with the sunrise and the sunset; it is a fact. You never say 'I agree with you that the sun rises in the east.' So could we perhaps put aside the sense of agreement and disagreement and inquire, without any bias or resistance, into whether there is actually individuality or whether there is something entirely different?

Our consciousness is the result of a million years or more. It contains all the animalistic, primitive essence, as we have come from the animal, from nature. Deep down in our consciousness we find that there are still the deep responses of the animals, the fears, and the desire for security. All that is part of our consciousness. Our consciousness also contains innumerable beliefs, faiths, reactions, actions, various memories, fear, pleasure, sorrow, and the search for complete security. All that is what we are. We may think part of us is divine, but that is also part of our thinking. All that consciousness, we think, belongs to each one of us. Right? Religions —Christianity, Hinduism, and others—have maintained that we are separate souls.

Now, we are questioning the whole of it. Do you not share the sorrow of the rest of human beings? Human beings throughout the world have various forms of fear and various forms of pleasure. They suffer as you suffer. They pray, they do all kinds of absurd ceremonies as you do, seeking stimulation, sensation through ceremonies as you do. So you share the consciousness of all humanity; you are the entire humanity. First see it logically. Every human being on this earth, whatever be his religion or belief, suffers. Every human being suffers, deeply or superficially, and tries to evade suffering. So this consciousness, which we have considered 'mine', this 'personal consciousness' is not a fact. Because all human beings living on this marvellous, beautiful earth—which we are carefully destroying —go through the same problems, the same pain, anxiety, loneliness, depression, tears, laughter, contradiction, and conflict between man and woman, husband and wife. So in your consciousness are you individuals? Because that is what you are: your consciousness. Whatever you think or imagine, whatever your tendencies, aptitudes, talents or gifts, all that is shared by all other human beings, who are exactly as you are, similar to you. This is a logical fact. And logic has a certain place, one must think clearly, logically, reasonably, sanely. But logic is based on thought. However logical one may be, thought is limited; thought may be reasonable but it is limited. So one must go beyond thought, beyond the limitation of reason and logic.

So you are the entire humanity; you are not an individual. Listen to that statement: you are the entire humanity, you are humanity, not an Indian and all that rubbish of division. When you listen to a statement of that kind, do you make an abstraction of it? That is, do you make an idea of the fact? The fact is one thing, and the idea about the fact another. The fact is that you have thought that you are individuals. Your religions, your daily life, your conditioning have made you believe that you are individuals. And somebody like the speaker comes along and says, 'Look carefully, is that so?' First you resist it saying, 'What are you talking about?' and push it aside. But if you listen carefully, then you share this statement that you are the entire humanity. How do you hear that statement—the sound of it? Do you make out of that statement an idea, away from the fact, and pursue the idea? You hear the statement that your consciousness, with all its reactions and actions, is shared by all humanity, because every human being goes through desperation, loneliness, sorrow, and pain as you do. How do you listen to that statement? Do you reject it, or do you examine it? Do you investigate it or merely say, 'What nonsense'? Which is it that you are doing—not tomorrow but now? What is your reaction to it? Either you listen to the depth of it, the sound of it, the beauty of it, the immensity of it, with its tremendous responsibility, or you treat it superficially, verbally, and say, 'Yes, I understand it intellectually.' Intellectual comprehension has very little meaning. It must be in your blood, in your guts, and out of that comes a different quality of the brain that is holistic, not fragmentary. It is the fragment that creates disorder. We, as individuals, have fragmented the human consciousness and therefore we live in disorder.

When you realize that you are the entire humanity—that is what love is. Then you will not kill another, you will not harm another. You will move out of all aggression, violence, and the brutality of religions. So our consciousness is one with all humanity. You don't see the beauty of it, the immensity of it. You will go back to your own pattern, thinking that you are all individuals, fighting, striving, competing, each trying to fulfil your own beastly little self. Yes, sir, this means nothing to you because you will go back to your own way of life. So it is much better not to listen to all this. If you listen to truth and don't act on it, it acts as poison. That is why our lives are so shoddy and superficial.

We must also talk over together why man perpetually seeks pleasure—pleasure in possession, pleasure in achievement, pleasure in power, pleasure in having a status. There is sexual pleasure, which is maintained by constant thinking about sex, imagining, picturing, and making images. That is, thought gives pleasure; sensation is turned into pleasure. So we must understand what pleasure is and why we seek it. We are not saying it is right or wrong. We are not condemning pleasure, as we are not condemning desire. Desire is part of pleasure. The fulfilment of desire is the very nature of pleasure. Desire may be the cause of disorder—each one wanting to fulfil his own particular desire.

So together we are going to investigate whether desire is one of the major causes of disorder; we must explore desire, not condemn it, not escape from it, not try to suppress it. Most religions have said, 'Suppress desire'—which is absurd. So let us look at it. What is desire? Put that question to yourself. Probably most of us have not thought about it at all. We have accepted it as a way of life, as the natural instinct of a man or a woman, and so we say, 'Why bother about it?'. Those people who have renounced the world, those who have entered monasteries, and so on try to sublimate their desires in the worship of a symbol or a person. Please bear in mind that we are not condemning desire. We are trying to find out what is desire, why man has, for millions of years, been caught not only physically but also psychologically in the trap of desire, in the network of desire.

Are you investigating with the speaker, or are you just listening to him while he explores or explains? You know, it is easy to be caught in explanations, in descriptions, and we are satisfied with the commentaries, descriptions, and explanations. We are not doing that here. I have to explain, describe, point out, put it in the framework of words, but you have to go into it too, and not just say, 'Yes, I agree', or 'I disagree.' You have to find out the nature of desire, its construction, how it is put together, and what its origin is.

The speaker will describe, not analyse. There is a difference between analysis and perception. Analysis implies the analyser and the thing to be analysed. Which means, the analyser is different from the analysed. But are they different? Suppose I am the analyser and I am envious. I begin to analyse why I am envious, as though I am different from envy. But envy is *me;* it is not separate from me. Greed, competition, comparison—all that is me. So we are not analysing; we are looking, hearing, and learning. Learning is not merely accumulating memory. That is necessary, but learning is something entirely different. It is not an accumulative process. In learning, you are moving, fresh, never recording.

So we are observing desire, its origin, and why human beings are caught in it endlessly. If you have a little money you want more. If you have a little power you want more. And power in any form, whether it be over your wife or your children, or political or religious power is an abominable thing. It is evil because it has nothing to do with truth. So what is the origin of desire? We live by sensation. If there was no sensation, biologically and psychologically, we would be dead human beings. Right? The cawing of that crow is acting on the eardrum and nerves, and the noise is translated as the cry of a crow. That is a sensation. Sensation is brought about by hearing or seeing, and then contact. You see a garden beautifully kept; the green is rich, perfect, and there are no weeds in it. It is a lovely thing to watch. There is the seeing. Then, if you are sensitive, you go and touch the grass. That is, seeing, contact, and then sensation. We live by sensation, it is necessary. If you are not sensitive, you are dull, you are half-alive, as most of us are. Take a very simple example. You see a nice sari or a shirt in a shop. You see it. You go inside and touch it; then there is the sensation of touching it and you say, 'By Jove, what lovely material that is.' Then what takes place after that? Are you waiting for me to tell you? Please do listen to this. If you see this for yourself, and not be told by another, then you become the teacher and the disciple. But if you repeat, repeat, repeat what somebody, including the speaker, has said, you remain mediocre, thoughtless, repetitive. So let's go into it. You see a beautiful car, you touch the polish, see its shape and texture. Out of that there is sensation. Then thought comes and says, 'How nice it would be if I got it, how nice it would be if I got into it and drove off.' So what has happened? Thought has intervened, has given shape to sensation. Thought has given to sensation the image of you sitting in the car and driving off. At that moment, at that second, when thought creates the image of you sitting in the car, desire is born. Desire is born when thought gives a shape, an image, to sensation. Now, sensation is the way of existence, it is part of existence. But you have learnt to suppress, conquer, or live with desire with all its problems. Now, if you understand this, not intellectually but actually, that when thought gives shape to sensation, at that second desire is born, then the question arises: Is it possible to see and touch the car—which is sensation—but not let thought create the image? So keep a gap. Do you understand this?

You see, one must also find out what is discipline. Because it is related to desire. The word 'discipline' comes from the word 'disciple'; the etymological meaning of that word is 'one who is learning'. A disciple is one who is learning—learning, and not conforming, not controlling, not suppressing, not obeying, not following. On the contrary, he is learning from observation. So you are learning about desire. Learning about it is not memorizing. Most of you are trained, especially if you are in the army, to discipline yourselves according to a pattern, trained to copy, follow, obey. That is what you are all doing, hoping that discipline will bring about order. But if you are learning, then that very learning becomes its own order; you don't need order imposed by law or anything else. So learn, find out, whether it is possible to allow sensation to flower and to not let thought interfere with it—to keep them apart. Will you do it? Then you will find that desire has its right place. And when you understand the nature of desire, there is no conflict about it.

We also ought to talk over together love, sorrow, and death. Please, all this is much too serious as it affects your daily life. This is not something you play with intellectually; it concerns your life—not somebody else's life—the way you live after all these million years. Look what your lives are, how empty, shallow, violent, brutal, inconsiderate, thoughtless. Look at it. All this has created such havoc in the world. You all want to have high positions, achieve something, become something. And seeing all this, there is great sorrow, isn't there? Every human being in this world, whether he is highly placed or is just an ignorant villager, goes through great sorrow. He may not recognize the nature and the beauty and the strength of sorrow, but he goes through pain like you do. Human beings have gone through sorrow for a million years. They haven't solved the problem; they want to escape from it. And what is the relationship of sorrow to love and death? Can there be an end to sorrow? This has been one of the questions mankind has asked for a million years. Is there an end to all the pain, the anxiety, the grief of sorrow?

Sorrow is not only your own particular sorrow; there is also the sorrow of mankind. Historically, there have been five thousand years of war. That means every year some people kill others for the sake of their tribe, their religion, their nation, their community, their individual protection, and so on. Have you ever realized what wars have done, the havoc they have created? How many millions have cried, how many millions have been wounded, left without arms, without legs, without eyes, even without a face? You people don't know anything about all this. So is there an end to sorrow and all the pain therein? And what is sorrow? Don't you know sorrow? Don't you? Are you ashamed to acknowledge it? When your son or daughter or somebody whom you think you love is taken away, don't you shed tears? Don't you feel terribly lonely because you have lost a companion forever? We are not talking about death but about this immense thing that man goes through without ever having a solution.

Without ending sorrow there is no love. Sorrow is part of your self-interest, part of your egotistic, self-centred activity. You cry for another, for your son, for your brother, for your mother. Why? Because you have lost something that you are attached to, something which gave you companionship, comfort, and all the rest of it. With the ending of that person, you realize how utterly empty, how lonely your life is. Then you cry. And there are many, many people ready to comfort you, and you slip very easily into that network, that trap, of comfort. There is the comfort in God, which is an image put together by thought, or comfort in some illusory concept or idea. And that's all you want. But you never question the very urge, the desire for comfort, never ask whether there is any comfort at all. One needs to have a comfortable bed or chair— that's all right. But you never ask whether there is any comfort at all psychologically, inwardly. Is it an illusion which has become your truth? You understand? An illusion can become your truth— the illusion that you are God, that there is God. That God has been created by thought, by fear. If you had no fear, there would be no God. God has been invented by man out of his fear, loneliness, despair, and the search for everlasting comfort. So you never ask whether there is comfort at all, which is deep, abiding satisfaction. You all want to be satisfied not only with the food that you eat, but also satisfied sexually, or by achieving some position of authority and having comfort in that position. So let us ask whether there is any comfort at all, whether there is anything that will be gratifying from the moment we are born till we die. Don't just listen to me; find out, give your energy, your thought, your blood, your heart to find out. And if there is no illusion, is there any comfort? If there is no fear, do you want comfort? Comfort is another form of pleasure.

So this is a very complex problem of our life— why we are so shallow, empty, filled with other people's knowledge and with books; why we are not independent, free human beings to find out; why we are slaves. This is not a rhetorical question; it is a question each one of us must ask. In the very asking and doubting, there comes freedom. And without freedom there is no sense of truth.

So we will go tomorrow into the question of what is a religious life and whether there is something that is totally sacred, holy, something not invented by thought.

*9 February 1985*

## TALK 4

*Is there a meditation that is not*
*brought about by thought?*

We were talking yesterday evening about sorrow and the ending of sorrow. With the ending of sorrow there is passion. Very few of us really understand or go deeply into the question of sorrow. Is it possible to end all sorrow? This has been a question that has been asked by all human beings, perhaps not very consciously; but deeply they have wanted to find out, as we all do, if there is an end to human suffering, human pain and sorrow. Because without the ending of sorrow, there is no love. When there is sorrow it is a great shock to the nervous system, like a blow to the whole physiological as well as psychological being. We generally try to escape from it by taking drugs or drink or through every form of religion. Or we become cynical or accept things as being inevitable.

Can we go into this question very deeply, seriously? Is it possible not to escape from sorrow at all? Perhaps my son dies, and there is immense sorrow, shock, and I discover that I am really a very lonely human being. I cannot face it, I cannot tolerate it. So I escape from it. And there are many escapes—mundane, religious, or philosophical. This escape is a waste of energy. Not to escape in any form from the ache, the pain of loneliness, the grief, the shock, but to remain completely with the event, with this thing called suffering—is that possible? Can we hold any problem—hold it and not try to solve it—try to look at it as we would hold a precious, exquisite jewel? The very beauty of the jewel is so attractive, so pleasurable that we keep looking at it. In the same way if we could hold our sorrow completely, without a movement of thought or escape, then that very action of not moving away from the fact brings about a total release from that which has caused pain. We will go into this a little later.

And we should also consider what is beauty. Beauty is very important—not the beauty of a person or of the marvellous paintings and statues in museums and ancient man's endeavour to express his feelings in stone or in paint or in poem. We should ask ourselves what is beauty. Beauty may be truth, beauty may be love. Without understanding the nature and the depth of that extraordinary word 'beauty', we may never be able to come upon that which is sacred. So we must go into the question of what is beauty.

When you see something greatly beautiful like a mountain full of snow against the blue sky, what actually takes place? When you see something extraordinarily alive, beautiful, majestic, for a moment, for a second, the very majesty of that mountain, the immensity of it drives away, puts aside all self-concern, all problems. At that second there is no 'me' watching it. The very greatness of the mountain drives away for a second all my self-concern. Surely one must have noticed this. Have you noticed a child with a toy? He has been naughty all day long—which is right—and you give him a toy, and then for the next hour, until he breaks it, he is extraordinarily quiet. The toy has absorbed his naughtiness, has taken him over. Similarly, when we see something extraordinarily beautiful, that very beauty absorbs us. That is, there is beauty when there is no self, no self-interest, no travail of the self. Without being absorbed or shaken by something extraordinarily beautiful like a mountain or a valley in deep shadow, without being taken over by the mountain, is it possible to understand beauty that is without the self? Because where there is the self there is no beauty, where there is self-interest there is no love. So love and beauty go together; they are not separate.

We have also to talk over together what is death. That is one certain thing that we all have to face. Whether we are rich or poor, ignorant or full of erudition, death is certain for every human being; we are all going to die. And we have never been able to understand the nature of death. We are always frightened of dying, aren't we? And we hope for continuity after death. So we are going to find out for ourselves what is death, because we are going to face it whether we are young or old. And to understand death, we must also inquire into what is living, what is our life.

Are we wasting our lives? By that word 'wasting' we mean dissipating our energy in various ways, dissipating it in specialized professions. Are we wasting our whole existence, our life? If you are rich you may say, 'Yes, I have accumulated a lot of money, it has been a great pleasure.' Or if you have a certain talent, that talent is a danger to a religious life. Talent is a gift, a faculty, an aptitude in a particular direction, which is specialization.

Specialization is a fragmentary process. So you must ask yourself whether you are wasting your life. You may be rich, you may have all kinds of faculties, you may be a specialist, a great scientist or a businessman, but at the end of your life has all that been a waste? All the travail, all the sorrow, all the tremendous anxiety, insecurity, the foolish illusions that man has collected, all his gods, all his saints and so on—have all that been a waste? You may have power, position, but at the end of it—what? Please, this is a serious question that you must ask yourself. Another cannot answer this question for you.

So we have separated living from dying. The dying is the end of our life. We put it as far away as possible—a long interval of time—but at the end of the long journey we die. And what is it that we call living? Earning money, going to the office from nine to five, over-worked either in a laboratory or in an office or in a factory, and the endless conflict, fear, anxiety, loneliness, despair, depression—this whole way of existence is what we call life, living. And to that we hold. But is that living? This living is pain, sorrow, anxiety, conflict, every form of deception, and corruption. Where there is self-interest there must be corruption. This is what we call living. We know that, we are very familiar with all that, that is our daily existence. And we are afraid of dying, which is to let go of all the things that we have known, all the things that we have experienced and gathered—the lovely furniture and the beautiful collection of pictures and paintings. And death comes and says, 'You cannot have any of those things any more.'

So we cling to the known, afraid of the unknown. We can invent reincarnation. But we never inquire into what it is that is born next life. What is born next life is a bundle of memories. Because we live by memories. We live by the knowledge we have acquired or inherited, and that knowledge is what we are. The self is the knowledge of the past experiences, thoughts, and so on. The self is that. The self may invent something divine in one. But it is still the activity of thought, and thought is always limited. So this is our living, this is what we call life—pleasure and pain, reward and punishment. And death means the ending of all that, the ending of all the things that we have thought, accumulated, enjoyed. And we are attached to all that. We are attached to our families, to all the accumulated money, to knowledge, to the beliefs and the ideals we have lived with. We are attached to all that. And death says, 'That's the end of it, old boy.'

Now, the question is: Why has the brain separated living—living which is conflict and so on—from death? Why has this division taken place? Does this division exist when there is attachment? Please, we are talking over things together, we are sharing this thing which man has lived with for a million years—the living and the dying. So we have to examine it together, and not resist, not say, 'Yes, I believe in reincarnation, that's what I live by, to me that is important.' Otherwise the conversation between us will come to an end. So we should really go into the question of what is living, what is wasting one's life, and what is dying. One is attached to so many things—to the guru, to accumulated knowledge, to the memory of one's son or daughter, and so on. That memory is you. Your whole brain is filled with memory—memory not only of recent events but also the deep abiding memory of that which has been the animal, the ape. We are part of that memory. We are attached to this whole consciousness. That's a fact.

And death comes and says, 'That is the end of your attachment.' So we are frightened of that, frightened of being *completely* free from all that. And death is that—the cutting off of *everything* that we have got. We can invent and say, 'I will continue next life.' But what is it that continues? You understand my question? What is it in us that desires to continue? Is there a continuity at all, except of your bank account, your going to the office every day, your routine of worship, and the continuity of your beliefs? They are all put together by thought. And the self, the 'me', the ego, the persona, is a bundle of complicated ancient and modern memories. You can see it for yourself. You don't have to study books and philosophies about all that. You can see for yourself very clearly that you are a bundle of memories. And death puts an end to all that memory. Therefore one is frightened.

Now, the question is: Can one live in the modern world with death? Not suicide—we are not talking about that. But can you, as you live, end all attachment, which *is* death? I am attached to the house I am living in, I have bought it, I have paid a great deal of money for it, and I am attached to all the furniture, the pictures, the family, the memories.

And death comes and wipes all that out. So can I live every day of my life with death? Ending *everything* every day, ending all your attachments—that's what it means to die. But we have separated living from dying. Therefore we are perpetually frightened. But when you bring life and death together, the living and the dying, then you will find out that there is a state of the brain in which all knowledge as memory ends. But you need knowledge to write a letter, to come here, to speak English, to keep accounts, to go home, and so on. You need knowledge but not knowledge as something that entirely occupies the mind.

We were talking the other day with a computer expert. The computer can be programmed and it stores that memory. It can also put aside all that memory on paper or a disc and keep itself empty so that it can be reprogrammed or instructed further. Similarly, can the brain use knowledge when necessary but be free of all knowledge? That is, our brain is recording all the time. You are recording what is being said now, and this record becomes a memory. That memory, that recording, is necessary in a certain area. That area is physical activity. Now, can the brain be free so that it can function totally in a different dimension? That is, *every* day, when you go to bed, wipe out *everything* that you have collected, die at the end of the day.

You hear a statement of this kind—that is, living is dying; they are not two separate things at all. You hear the statement not only with the hearing of the ear, but if you listen carefully, you also hear the truth of it, the actuality of it, and for the moment you see the clarity of it. Later on, you slip back—you are attached, you know all the rest of it. So is it possible for each one of you to die at the end of the day to everything that is not necessary, to every memory of hurt, to your beliefs, your faiths, your anxieties, your sorrow? End all that every day and then you will find that you are living with death all the time—death being the ending.

One should also go into the question of ending. We never end anything completely. We end if there is some profit in it, if there is some reward. Can we voluntarily end without the assumption that there is something better in the future? And it is possible to live that way in the modern world. That is a holistic way of living in which there is the living and the dying taking place all the time.

Then we ought to also talk over together what is love. Is love sensation? Is love desire? Is love pleasure? Is love put together by thought? Do you love your wife or your husband or your children—love? Is love jealousy? Don't say 'no' because you *are* jealous. Is love fear, anxiety, pain, and all the rest of it? So what is love? You may be very rich, you may have power, position, importance, all that hierarchical outlook on life, but without love, without that quality, that perfume, that flame, you are just an empty shell. If you loved your children, would there be wars? If you loved your children, would you allow them to maim themselves through wars, kill others, hurt another? Can love exist where there is ambition? Please, you have to face all this. But you don't because you are caught in a routine, in a repetition of sensation as sex, and so on. Love has nothing whatsoever to do with pleasure, with sensation. Love is not put together by thought. Therefore it is not within the structure of the brain; it is something entirely outside the brain. While the brain by its very nature and structure is an instrument of sensation, nervous responses, and so on, love cannot exist where there is mere sensation. Memory is not love.

We should also talk over together what is a religious life and what is religion, though it is a very complex question. Man has always sought, has inquired into, has longed for something beyond the physical, beyond the everyday existence of pain and sorrow and pleasure. He has always sought something beyond—first in the clouds, in the thunder as the voice of God. Then he worshipped trees and stones. The primitives still do; in the villages far away from these ugly, beastly towns they still worship stones, trees, and small images. Man wants to find out if there is something sacred. And the priest comes along and says, 'I will point out to you, I will show you'—just as the guru does. And there are the rituals of the Western priests, their repetition, and the worship of their particular image. And you too have your own images. Or you may not believe in any of that; you may, 'I am an atheist, I do not believe in God, I am a humanitarian.' But man has always wanted to find out something that may be beyond time, beyond all thought.

So we are going to inquire, exercise our brains, our reason and our logic to find out what is religion, what is a religious life. Is a religious life possible in this modern world? Which does not mean becoming

71

a monk or joining an organized group of monks. We will be able to find out for ourselves what is really, truly, a religious life only when we understand what religions actually are and put aside all that, and not belong to *any* religion, to any organized religion, to any guru, and not have any psychological or so-called spiritual authority. There is no spiritual authority *whatsoever*. That is one of the crimes that we have committed—we have invented the mediator between truth and ourselves.

So you begin to inquire into what is religion, and in the very process of that inquiry you are living a religious life, not at the end of it. In the very process of looking, watching, discussing, doubting, questioning, and having no belief or faith, you are already living a religious life. We are going to do that now.

We seem to lose all reason, all logic and sanity when it comes to religious matters. So we have to be logical, rational; we have to doubt, to question. All the things man has put together—the gods, the saviours, the gurus and their authority—all that is not religion. That is merely the assumption of authority by the few. Or you *give* them authority. Have you ever noticed that where there is disorder socially or politically, there comes a dictator, a ruler? We have recently had examples of this—in Mussolini, and in Hitler, that mad man. Where there is disorder politically, religiously, or in our life, we create authority. You are responsible for the authority. And there are people who are only too willing to accept that authority.

So together we are going to look at what is religion. Where there is fear, man inevitably seeks something that will protect him, safeguard him, that will hold him in a sense of certainty, complete security, because he is basically frightened. Out of that fear, we invent gods, out of that fear we invent all the rituals, all the circus that goes on in the name of religion. All the temples in this country, all the churches and the mosques are put together by thought. You may say that there is direct revelation, but you never question, doubt that revelation; you accept it. And if one uses logic and reason, one sees that all the superstitions that one has accumulated is not religion. Obviously. Can you put all that aside to find out what is the nature of religion, of the mind that holds the quality of religious living?

Can we, as human beings who are frightened, not invent, not create illusions but face fear? Fear can disappear completely when you hold it, remain with it, not escape from it, when you give your whole attention to it. It is like a light being thrown on fear, a great, flashing light. Then that fear disappears completely. And when there is no fear there is no god, there are no rituals; all that becomes unnecessary, stupid. All that is irreligious. The things that thought has invented are irreligious, because thought is merely a material process based on experience, knowledge, and memory. And thought invents the whole rigmarole, the whole structure of organized religions, which have no meaning at all. Can you put aside all that voluntarily, without seeking a reward at the end of it? Will you do it? When you do that, then you begin to ask: What is religion, and is there something beyond all time and thought?

You may ask that question but if thought invents something beyond, then it is still a material process. We have said that thought is a material process because it is sustained, nourished, in the brain cells. The speaker is not a scientist, but you can watch it in yourself, watch the activity of your own brain, which is the activity of thought. So if you can put aside all that easily, without any resistance, then you inevitably ask: 'Is there something beyond all time and space? Is there something that has never before been seen by any man? Is there something immensely sacred? Is there something that the brain has never touched?' You will find that out if you have taken the first step—which is to wipe away all this rubbish called religion by using your brain, by your logic, your doubt, your questioning.

Then what is meditation? That is part of so-called religion. What is meditation? Is it to escape from the noise of the world? To have a silent mind, a quiet mind, a peaceful mind? And you practise systems, methods, to become aware, to keep your thoughts under control. You sit cross-legged and repeat some mantra. I am told that the etymological meaning of that word 'mantra' is 'ponder over not-becoming'. That is one of the meanings. And it also means 'absolve, put aside all self-centred activity'. That is the real, root meaning of mantra. But we repeat, repeat, repeat, and carry on with our self-interest, our egoistic ways, and so mantra has lost its meaning. So what is meditation? Is meditation a conscious effort? We meditate consciously, practise in order to achieve something, to achieve a quiet mind, a sense of stillness of the brain. What is the difference between that meditator and the man who says, 'I want money, so I will work for it'? What is the difference between the two? Both are seeking an achievement, aren't they? One is called spiritual achievement, the other is called mundane achievement. But they are both in the line of achievement. So, to the speaker, that is not meditation at all. Any conscious, deliberate, active desire with its will is not meditation.

So one has to ask: Is there a meditation that is not brought about by thought? Is there a meditation which you are not aware of? Any deliberate process of meditation is not meditation; that is so obvious. You can sit cross-legged for the rest of your life, meditate, breathe and do all that business, but you will not come anywhere near the other thing. Because all that is a deliberate action to achieve a result—the cause and the effect. But the effect becomes the cause. So it is a cycle you are caught in. So is there a meditation that is not put together by desire, by will, by effort? The speaker says there is. You don't have to believe it. On the contrary, you must doubt it, question it as the speaker has questioned it, doubted it, torn it apart. Is there a meditation that is not contrived, organized? To go into that, we must understand the brain which is conditioned, limited. And that brain is trying to comprehend the limitless, the immeasurable, the timeless—if there is such a thing as the timeless.

And for that, it is important to understand sound. Sound and silence go together. You don't understand sound, the depth of sound, but you have separated sound from silence. Sound is the word, sound is your heart beating. The universe—universe in the sense of the whole earth, all the heavens, the million stars, the whole sky—is filled with sound. Obviously. You don't have to listen to scientists about it. And we have made that sound into something intolerable. So we want to have a brain that is quiet, peaceful. But when you listen to sound, the very listening is the silence. Silence and sound are not separate.

So meditation is something that is not contrived, organized. Meditation begins at the first step, which is to be free of all your psychological hurts, free of all your accumulated fears, anxieties, loneliness, despair, and sorrow. That is the foundation. That is the first step, and the first step is the last step. If you take that first step, it is over. But we are unwilling to take that first step because we don't want to be free. We want to depend—on power, on other people, on environment, on our experience and knowledge. You are always depending, depending, and are never free of all dependence, all fear. Therefore the ending of sorrow is love. Where there is that love there is compassion. And that compassion has its own integral intelligence. And when that intelligence acts, its action is always true. There is no conflict where there is that intelligence.

You have heard all this. You have heard about the ending of fear, the ending of sorrow, and about beauty and love. But the hearing is one thing, and action is another. You have heard all these things which are true, logical, sane, rational, but you won't act according to that. You will go home and begin all over again—your worries, your conflicts, your miseries. So one asks, 'What is the point of it all? What is the point of listening to the speaker and not living it?' The listening and not doing it is a waste of your life. If you listen to something that is the truth and do not act, you are wasting your life. And life is much too precious. It is the only thing that we have. And we have also lost touch with nature, which means we have lost touch with ourselves, which is part of nature. You do not love the trees, the birds, the waters, the mountains. We are destroying the earth. And we are destroying each other. All that is such a waste of life. When one realizes all this, not merely intellectually or verbally, then one lives a religious life. To put on a loincloth or to go around begging or to join a monastery— that is not a religious life. The religious life begins when there is no conflict, when there is this sense of love. Then you can love another, your wife or your husband, but that love is shared by all human beings. It is not given to one person and is therefore not restricted.

So, if you give your heart and mind and brain, there is something that is beyond all time. And there is the benediction of that. Not in temples, not in churches, not in mosques. That benediction is where you are.

*10 February 1985*

Further information regarding Krishnamurti books, audio and video tapes, and CDs can be obtained from:

Krishnamurti Foundation India
Vasanta Vihar, 124 Greenways Road
Chennai—600 028
E-mail: publications@kfionline.org
Website: http://www.kfionline.org

Krishnamurti Foundation Trust Ltd
Brockwood Park, Bramdean
Hampshire S024 OLQ, U.K.
E-mail: info@brockwood.org.uk

Krishnamurti Foundation of America
P.O. Box 1560
Ojai, California 93024-1560, U.S.A
E-mail: kfa@kfa.org

Fundacion Krishnamurti Latinoamericana
No. 59, 1 Ext.D, 28015
Madrid, Spain
E-mail: anadonfk@ddnet.es